Have you…
HAD IT WITH AN "ADDICT"?

Love Wins
PRAYERS
When You Don't Know How to Pray

You Are Not Alone

Cheryl Shelton Iaquinta

Scripture noted:

MSG The Message Bible - NKJ New King James Bible

ICB International Children's Bible - NAS New American Standard Bible

NLT New Living Translation Bible - NIV New International Version Bible

AMP Amplified Bible

Definitions in Glossary of Terms are from:

Google, Urban and Merriam-Webster Dictionaries

Author: Cheryl Shelton Iaquinta

Edited by: Shannon Stockstill

Cover image by: Jazella from Pixabay

Published by: Friend of Love Publishing

Copyright © 2019 Cheryl Shelton Iaquinta

Prayer, Recovery, Spiritual & Inspirational

All rights reserved.

DEDICATION

This book is dedicated to my son Clay.
My love and respect for you are eternal.
Your love is more alive today than yesterday.
I am grateful that God gave me you!

Momma

Table of Contents

Chapter 1	The Way I See It	1
Chapter 2	The Blood	12
Chapter 3	Forgiveness	15
Chapter 4	Eyes to See	18
Chapter 5	Ears to Hear	21
Chapter 6	Heart to Love	24
Chapter 7	Physical Health	27
Chapter 8	Mental Health	30
Chapter 9	Spiritual Health	33
Chapter 10	Words	36
Chapter 11	Environment	39
Chapter 12	Safety	42
Chapter 13	People	45
Chapter 14	Recovery Programs	48
Chapter 15	Jobs	51
Chapter 16	Pride	54
Chapter 17	Trust	57
Chapter 18	Church	60
Chapter 19	Deception	63
Chapter 20	Family	66

Chapter 21	Legal Matters	69
Chapter 22	Children	72
Chapter 23	Emotions	75
Chapter 24	Addiction	78
	In Loving Memory	81
	Closing	82
	Glossary of Terms	83
	Resources	86

ACKNOWLEDGMENTS

To my husband who has walked by my side, I love you. We have had good times and some bad yet by the grace of God we are still one for which I am grateful. God has sustained and grown our love through this journey in a way that cannot be put into words, only experienced.

LOVE WINS

The prayers contained within, would not be possible if not for all our friends and family that have carried us with prayer, fasting, sleepless nights, tears of pain, love and those of joy. I am eternally grateful to all of you, those that have walked close by as well as those who have prayed from afar.

I am certain that you were sent from heaven above to pray when I did not know how.

FOREWARD

About the Author

The following scriptures are the best words from our Lord and Savior, her earthly family and friends to describe His daughter Cheryl Shelton Iaquinta.

She is strong and is respected by the people. She looks forward to the future with joy. She speaks wise words and she teaches others to be kind. She watches over her family and she is always busy. Her children bless her. Her husband also praises her. Charm can fool you, and beauty can trick you. But a woman who respects the Lord should be praised. Proverbs 31:25-28, 30 ICB

And though a man might prevail against one who is alone, two will withstand him-a threefold cord is not quickly broken. Ecclesiastes 4:12 ESV

Cheryl is a loving wife and mother, an ordained minister, and friend to many. She has spent her life loving Jesus, serving and loving others, and most importantly praying her son into eternity with Jesus.

I joined her 4 years ago in a journey of intercession with the Lord as our 3 stranded cord. This journey was to pray for her son Clay, and his battle with heroin. I watched her transformation from living and praying in fear of Clay's addiction to boldly loving and believing in the grace that leaves the 99 and chases the 1 to save him.

Through this journey of interceding, Cheryl never wavered in her belief that love wins.

With wise words and through wisdom, Cheryl provides a healing opportunity to pray for those who aren't always easy to love while in addiction. She offers a hand to hold and a window into her story of how she prayed for her beloved son. These prayers offer hope to the one who feels alone and hopeless. These prayers will bring peace to the troubled heart.

In joining this journey on the following pages, be prepared to know the heart of God and to love the addict in front of you. Cheryl didn't know the outcome as no one does, but she did know that no matter the outcome…LOVE WINS.

Be blessed as you read,

Shannon Stockstill

FINALLY, BE STRONG IN THE LORD AND IN HIS MIGHTY POWER. PUT ON THE WHOLE ARMOR OF GOD, SO THAT YOU CN TAKE YOUR STAND AGAINST THE DEVIL'S SCHEMES.
EPHESIANS 6:10-11

FOR GOD IS NOT THE AUTHOR OF CONFUSION,
BUT OF PEACE.
1 CORINTHIANS 14:33

THERE ARE THREE THINGS THAT WILL ENDURE, FAITH, HOPE AND LOVE AND THE GREATEST OF THESE IS LOVE.
1 CORINTHIANS 13:13

YOU WERE NEVER MEANT TO GO THIS ALONE…

OUR TESTIMONY

THEY (WE) HAVE DEFEATED HIM BY THE BLOOD OF THE LAMB AND BY THEIR (OUR) TESTIMONY. AND THEY (WE) DID NOT LOVE THEIR (OUR) LIFE, EVEN WHEN FACED WITH DEATH.

REVELATION 12:11

CHAPTER 1

THE WAY I SEE IT

o·ri·en·ta·tion
noun (physical definition)
"awareness of one's environment as to time, space, objects and persons"

My experience with addiction is that of a mother. One absolute truth that I have found necessary for survival in the throws of addiction, was being aware that I was not alone. Addiction tries to keep you hidden in blame, shame and guilt. The lock on the door is fear. If you don't have someone to pray with, you do now! Hold on, you are not alone.

Be determined to keep your focus on God and position yourself with others that will pray, for you and with you.

You will notice through this writing that I have the word "addict" in quotation marks. It is important to know that I consider this a condition that affects the mind, it doesn't speak to someone's heart, it is *not who someone actually is.* I believe that addiction is a condition and circumstance that can be overcome. Why? It is not God's design for anyone to struggle with addiction and it is never intended to be a part of anyone's purpose or destiny.

God has a specific plan for each one of us and it is good. Our lives change through experiences and with choices that we make. Our choices have consequences, but that doesn't change what God says about who we are, even if sometimes, He's the only one who can see it.

"Addicts" make decisions completely against who they are. The person addicted, as well as their family and friends may lose sight of their very nature, their character, and their heart. But, here's the thing…God is steadfast. He never changes. He knows the nature, character and heart of the person struggling with addiction and He knows the nature, character and heart of those that love them.
God loves us to life as our Creator and He loves us to life everlasting as we pass from this earth into eternity.

In December of 2018 our son had just finished five months in a recovery program. Nine days after he was home, on December 21st, he took a lethal dose of heroin mixed with fentanyl that took his life here on earth.

For the prior eight years, we had been filled with information from counselors, meetings, rehabilitation programs and people who had dealt with addiction and it was not until this happened that I realized, it had one purpose, death. That's where Jesus stepped in. He overcame death! His overwhelming love for Clay reached for him in that moment and Clay overcame death too!

I have experienced a love that brings a reckoning to heaven and earth. I am certain, love wins. God's love and mercy stepped in that night. God is the only one who knew Clay's battle and we know we will see him again.

In the aftermath of the tears, hugs, calls, texts and prayers, I received one message that compelled me to write this book. A dear friend of over 15 years who had prayed for countless hours, days and years for Clay and our family sent me a text a few days later, it read:

"Morning sister - I gotta tell ya, I've been just a bit angry with all of this. I mean if anyone's son should have made it...yours should have. The way you prayed for him, prayed for others - not taking "no" for an answer. Continuing to seek, continuing to knock. I scream why God why?!? And I kid you not, this huge rush of peace overwhelms me and I feel/hear. "It's because she did pray...that he made it." Clay never could have made it through all that noise, all those distractions, without all your prayers grounding him, centering him, covering him. The pull of addiction is strong...but your prayers my friend were stronger. You rent the heavens on his behalf and he/He heard. Through it all...Jesus was with Clay. And He is with you too...through it all."
A.W.

A huge "rush of peace" overwhelmed me as I began to picture all the friends and family that had prayed over the years. Hundreds and thousands of prayers, no doubt…I am sure this is true. The words, "thank you" will never be enough. Clay, overtaken by the stronghold of addiction, made a decision that took his life here on earth, not a decision to take his life. This addiction did not disqualify him from heaven! The prayers prayed on his behalf and his love for Jesus paved the way for his eternal life in heaven.

Jerimiah 29: 11-13 MSG
The Lord's Decree
"I'll show up and take care of you as I promised and bring you back home. I know what I'm doing. I have it all planned out. Plans to take care of you, not abandon you, plans to give you the future you hope for. When you call on me, when you come and pray to me, I'll listen. When you come looking for me, you'll find me. "

I've always heard and believed God's plan was good. I didn't fully grasp until now that God's highest good for every soul is when He meets us face to face as we enter eternity. My perception was very finite and contained within the earthly realm of a mother's heart. I always saw "future" as an earthly future. A future somehow attached to earthly dreams and my own perception like, marriage, children, homes, cars, dream job's, great family and friends.

God's perspective is so much bigger!

His perspective is eternal and not attached to this earth.

In those last few years through Clay's addiction, I came to realize, I could trust God for everyone else but I had trouble trusting Him for myself. God, through His overwhelming love pursued me and my total trust in Him. I didn't know how to trust like that. I chose God over and over and over but never fully surrendered the worry in my "mother's heart" to Him. I fought surrendering Clay to God, like I was protecting him. It was the hardest thing I'd ever done but with God's help, I finally realized God loved him more than I ever could. It was in the letting go that I began to see Clay's heart again…straight through the chaos. What a gift! I am forever grateful that God didn't give up on me. His love pursued me and His love won.

I have met many wonderful people from all walks of life that have battled addiction and loved deeply those that it has touched. Its victims are young and old and of every race, color and creed.

I am very grateful to be able to say that I have met many who have overcome addiction through the power of prayer, the Word of God and the love of Jesus. I have also experienced God's ability to reach through the dimensions of heaven and earth to fulfill the purpose and destiny of someone who no longer lives here with us, but eternally with Him. Death does not stop the will of God. The power of His love is unstoppable.

LOVE WINS

I fully believe that God knew you would find your way here and that He is already positioned to answer every petition lifted to His ear. Hold on, He is here to help!

Several years ago, I worked as a flight attendant and there was a "rule of wisdom" that we taught at the beginning of each flight. I'm sure you've heard it before…

"If the oxygen mask is deployed, put yours on first, then you can help the person next to you".

Prayer, can be like oxygen!
I'd like to pray for you.

Lord, I pray that you would put your arms around the one reading this prayer. You know far more than I, what they need. I pray that you would touch their spirit first, so that they may receive all that you have for them. Let them experience your presence right where they are. Impress upon their hearts Oh Lord that there is no reason to be ashamed or feel lack in anyway, having found themselves in this place. Tell them Lord, they are not alone. Show them that You are there through every high and every low. Send them Godly friends that will pray *for* them and *with* them and Lord, do whatever it takes to insure they know that you are real and that you care about what & who they care about. Give them wisdom, knowledge and understanding of your ways so that they do not depend upon themselves or any other voice that tries to bring correction or guidance without going through you first. I ask you to give them an extra measure of faith and prepare them for the time that they are about to spend with you. Lord, I stand in the gap for this one, believing with them and when necessary for them for miracles. Miracles of deliverance, salvation and eternal life. Lord, prepare the way so that they encounter you with every step they take and every word they pray. Give them hope Lord, let them see, touch, taste, smell and hear that your presence is a gamechanger. Cause them to experience the power of prayer today!

Intervene Lord!
Let today be a gamechanger for this one!
IN JESUS MIGHTY NAME, AMEN

I don't want you to miss a moment of this encounter. If you have not asked Jesus to be Lord of your life, please don't miss this opportunity to do it. The power to overcome everything you are facing is in the name of Jesus. This is where the power to overcome begins. You can revisit this page as often as you like…

If you do know Jesus, pray along with us! There are many people that may be reading these words for the first time and I have asked God to allow us to all intercede for each other as we read this together.

This is our prayer…You alone can choose that it be yours.

Lord, I come to you today in need.
I can no longer carry the weight of this world and the things in my life. My heart is broken, and I am weak in body and spirit.
I need you Jesus, son of God to take over.
I am asking you to take it all. I give you my heart, my soul, my mind and my body. I give you my lack of understanding and all of my doubt. I no longer want to go this alone; I need you. Please forgive me for words I have spoken and things I have done that were not done in love. I am asking you, Jesus to be Lord of my life. Help me love like you.
Amen

If this is the first time you have asked Jesus to come into your life and take over, write down the date!
_____/_____/_____

Things are about to change.

The power to move mountains, part the seas, stop the sun in the sky, heal the sick and make the impossible possible, is at hand. My heart is full of hope for you because I believe God is going to move on your behalf and show you mighty things. It's important to remember that God's "way" doesn't always look like we think it will. Don't set yourself up by predetermining what you expect to encounter, just know, God has your highest good in the palm of His hands, He is an ever-present help in times of trouble and He cares about everything and everyone you care about. God has a way of using the things that look the worst to work things out for the very best. As we take our positions to pray remember: You can't mess this up. God will do the work…we just pray. We pray together.

<u>Prayer is not about a feeling or emotion, it's simply about the choice to pray. Choose to pray, don't give up.</u>

in·ter·cede *(verb)*
"to intervene on behalf of another"

We intercede on behalf of others when they cannot ask for themselves! Prayer penetrates the atmosphere and engages the spirit. Prayer touches those things we cannot see and puts into motion *"help"* we cannot explain.

Ephesians 6:12 AMP

12 For our struggle is not against flesh and blood [contending only with physical opponents], but against the rulers, against the powers, against the world forces of this [present] darkness, against the spiritual forces of wickedness in the heavenly (supernatural) places.

Isaiah 59:19 KJB

When the enemy shall come in like a flood, the Spirit of the Lord shall lift up a standard against him.

Intercession
Positioning Ourselves to Pray

There are so many opinions about how to pray, what to pray and who can pray. I'm here to tell you, anybody can pray. No position or claim to Christ is greater for one than any other. God wants you to know you can freely come to Him in prayer. You can pray for someone that doesn't know God. You can pray for someone that's running from God. You can pray for someone who denounces God. Pray too, for His children and pray for yourself.

Sometimes, it takes a minute to grasp His great love. He is listening and ready to act on your behalf. You are loved! You are worth it! The one(s) you are praying for are loved, don't give up…they are worth it!

Hebrews 10:19-23 ICB
Continue to Trust God

19 So, brothers (and sisters), we are completely free to enter the Most Holy Place. We can do this without fear because of the blood of Jesus' death. 20 We can enter through a new way that Jesus opened for us. It is a living way. It leads through the curtain— Christ's body. 21 And we have a great priest over God's house. 22 So let us come near to God with a sincere heart and a sure faith. We have been cleansed and made free from feelings of guilt. And our bodies have been washed with pure water. 23 Let us hold firmly to the hope that we have confessed.

<u>*We can trust God to do what He promised*</u>.

As we pray through this book together, place your loved one's name in the blank of every prayer. You may want to make a list of names…those blanks get full fast!

<u>Hearing</u> *the words of a prayer, changes things.*

Tip: There is an extra measure of faith injected into our minds and hearts through the *hearing* of prayer. If you have never prayed out loud, I encourage you to try it! When you speak into your atmosphere, it changes things. I can't explain it. It must be experienced.

THERE IS POWER IN THE SPOKEN WORD

The pages titled "BY CLAY'S OWN HAND" are prayers, thoughts and conclusions taken from his recovery journal.

THE BLOOD

"BUT IF WE WALK IN THE LIGHT AS HE IS IN THE LIGHT, WE HAVE FELLOWSHIP WITH ONE ANOTHER, AND THE BLOOD OF JESUS CHRIST HIS SON CLEANSES US FROM ALL SIN." ~1 JOHN 1:7

LORD, WE COME TO YOU ON BEHALF OF _____ ASKING THAT YOU COVER HIM/HER IN THE BLOOD OF JESUS. PLACE A BLOOD LINE AROUND HIM/HER THAT THE ENEMY CANNOT CROSS. PROTECT HIM/HER FROM EVERY ASSIGNMENT THAT HAS BEEN PLACED UPON HIM/HER FROM BIRTH, THROUGH EVERY SEASON OF LIFE, AND EVEN GENERATIONS. KEEP HIM/HER AS HE/SHE MAKES HIS/HER WAY OUT OF THE CHAOS & CONFUSION AND THE DECEPTION & DARKNESS OF ADDICTION AND INTO A PLACE OF LIGHT AND TRUTH.

PROTECT HIM/HER LORD, EVEN FROM HIMSELF/HERSELF.

WE CALL YOU LORD, TO REMEMBRANCE THAT THE BLOOD OF JESUS BOUGHT _____ REDEMPTION. REDEEM HIM/HER FROM EVERY CIRCUMSTANCE AND DECISION THAT OPPOSES GOOD. PURSUE HIM/HER JESUS UNTIL HE/SHE ACKNOWLEDGES YOU AS HIS/HER LORD AND SAVIOR. TODAY, WE ASK YOU TO INTERVENE!

SAVE HIM/HER LORD, FROM THE GRIP OF ADDICTION.
SEVER THE TIE THAT BINDS HIM/HER TO IT FOREVER.
LET THIS PRAYER BE HEARD THROUGHOUT HEAVEN.
LET OUR PETITION BE KNOWN TO ALL.
LET EVERY ADVERSARY HEAR AND KNOW THAT, _____ BELONGS TO YOU THE LORD GOD ALMIGHTY, CREATOR OF ALL THINGS!

AMEN

Names, Notes and New Things

1-16-20 Today I claim Annice for You. I claim Your victory through the Power of Your Blood. Thank You for the work You are doing.

2-17-20 Father she needs You. She dwells in darkness with her love - drugs & sex. Please don't let this be the end of the story

FROM CLAY'S OWN HAND...
Journal Entry

God, as I begin this new portion of my life, help me to let go of any offenses that I may still be holding on to. Help me to be more like you. Help me to be more forgiving.

Wisdom from God is always pure, it seeks things that are naturally good, it is always gentle and willing to yield to others.

FORGIVENESS
"...AND FORGIVE US OUR DEBTS AS WE FORGIVE OUR DEBTORS" ~MATTHEW 6:12

OH GOD, THERE ARE SO MANY WOUNDS AND BROKEN HEARTS IN THE WAKE OF ADDICTION, HELP US FORGIVE EACH OTHER.

HELP ME FORGIVE MYSELF AND HELP ME FORGIVE _____ . WE PRAY OH LORD THAT YOU WILL HELP OUR UNFORGIVENESS. WE PRAY THAT YOU WOULD HELP _____ FORGIVE THOSE WHO HAVE HURT HIM/HER. WE PRAY LORD THAT YOU WOULD OPEN _____ HEART AND MIND SO THAT HE/SHE CAN ALSO FORGIVE HIMSELF/HERSELF FOR THINGS HE/SHE HAS SAID AND DONE THAT HURT OTHERS. REACH DEEP INTO HIS/HER HEART AND BY YOUR SPIRIT HEAL THE WOUNDS THAT HAVE BEEN INFLICTED BY BLAME, SHAME AND GUILT. DELIVER HIM/HER OH LORD FROM THE HEAVINESS AND THE HOPELESSNESS THAT HAVE BEEN POURED INTO HIS/HER THROUGH UNFORGIVENESS AND REVERSE THE FLOOD GATES. YES, OH LORD, REVERSE THE FLOOD GATES. LET THE PAIN AND HURT FLOW OUT OF HIM/HER LIKE A RIVER. RELEASE HIM/HER OH LORD THROUGH THE FORGIVENESS OF HIMSELF/HERSELF AND THEN THE FORGIVENESS OF EVERYONE THAT HAS HARMED HIM/HER ALONG THE WAY. GIVE HIM/HER THE ABILITY TO SEE AND UNDERSTAND THAT HURTING PEOPLE, HURT PEOPLE AND THAT THROUGH YOUR LOVE, HE/SHE HAS THE ABILITY TO ESCAPE THIS DEATH TRAP CALLED UNFORGIVENESS. GIVE HIM/HER EYES TO SEE, IT IS NOT HIM/HER, BUT YOU AND YOU ALONE THAT MAKES THIS POSSIBLE AND LET HIM/HER EXPERIENCE...YOU, MAKING ALL THINGS NEW. JESUS, RELEASE HIM/HER!

AMEN

Names, Notes and New Things

2/18/20 Father, I do pray that You would help Annie to forgive herself and others. She carries so much guilt and blame. Help me to forgive her too.

FROM CLAY'S OWN HAND...
Journal Entry

God, whatever walls I have built up, that I cannot see, help me to break them down and whatever I cannot see, help me to realize.

Lord, help me to keep focused on you and to be a leader and servant for you.

EYES TO SEE

"I pray that the eyes of your heart may be enlightened so that you will know what is the hope of His calling." ~Ephesians 1:18

Lord, today we ask that You give _____ eyes to see the way out of addiction. Touch his/her mind's eye, as well as his/her physical eyes, removing every veil and distraction that has stopped him/her from being able to see clearly. Lord, open _____ eyes. Open his/her spiritual eyes, open his/her natural eyes. Let _____ see with new eyes. Help him/her see past everything in his/her environment, through the noise and past everything going on in the atmosphere, straight through to You... the WAY out. Let _____ see and know who his/her enemies are and who has been strategically placed by the enemy to divert his/her path towards death and destruction.

But...Oh Lord, let him/her also see that You are there. Let him/her see that You have also placed people strategically, to help him/her see the path that You have created especially for him/her. A path to life. Show him/her those You have sent to help him/her navigate YOUR WAY out. Help him/her see the hand of the one who is there to lead him/her and guide him/her to safety, even if it is an angel. Oh Lord, help him/her see the illumination You have placed along his/her path, showing him/her the WAY. Give _____ eyes to see YOU today. Open the eyes of his/her heart and cause him/her to see that You have made a way out!

Amen

Names, Notes and New Things

2/19/20 Oh Father, please show Annie the way out. Please show her the path that You have made through the wilderness. Please send someone to guide her. Please send angels to guard and guide her away from the path of destruction she is on. Thank You.

FROM CLAYS OWN HAND...
Journal Entry

Dear God, please allow me to hear you in all things so that you may guide me in all situations.

God, reveal your plan for my life so that I can live out your plan for my life.

My motivation for serving Christ is to become the man that God sees in me.

My confidence rests in God and Jesus Christ.

EARS TO HEAR

He whose ear listens to the life-giving reproof, Will dwell among the wise. ~Proverbs 15:31 NAS

Lord, we come to You today, asking that You would open _____ ears. Cause him/her to hear Your voice. Cause him/her to hear a new sound. Speak Oh Lord, directly to _____ spirit, LET HIM/HER HEAR! As this world is full of noise, stop it in its tracks and let _____ only hear Your voice and the voices of those You have sent. Let him/her hear of Your love, let him/her hear of Your goodness, let him/her hear of Your plan to redeem everything in his/her life. Let him/her hear that there is nothing too big for You, no nothing! Tell him/her that You have seen and heard everything that pertains to his/her life and You love him/her with an everlasting love anyway.

Let him/her hear that there is nothing that can separate him/her from Your love and that You are able to change everything. Let him/her hear the testimonies of those You have already redeemed from addiction. Let him/her hear the testimonies of those You have already redeemed from legal matters. Let him/her hear the testimonies of those You have already redeemed from health issues caused by addiction and let him/her hear that there is nothing too hard for You. Let him/her hear You are able to repair the breech between him/her and all his/her family and friends. Let him/her hear that You are able…in all things. Cause him/her to hear and believe that nothing is impossible with You.

Amen

Names, Notes and New Things

1/20/20 Father, please bring to Annie's mind good memories of love and laughter. Help her to see clearly her path of destruction and help her choose to get on the path to health - mental, spiritual, emotional and ~~spiritual~~ physical. Remind her of how much I love her and have been there for her. Please bring godly people into her life. Help her to be desperate for you and to find you and the help she needs. Please work in her life. Please remove the bad influences and replace them with good. Please remove all desire she has for drugs and alcohol and replace them with a desire for you.

FROM CLAY'S OWN HAND...
Journal Entry

Father give me patience not to judge those who are doing your work when they slip up as I have so many times.

God, help me to remove the speck from my own eye and to be forgiving of others mistakes.

Forgiveness is the key to compassion.

HEART TO LOVE

"A NEW COMMAND I GIVE YOU: LOVE ONE ANOTHER. AS I HAVE LOVED YOU, SO YOU MUST LOVE ONE ANOTHER." ~ JOHN 13:34

OH GOD, GIVE ME A HEART TO LOVE. HELP ME TO LOVE LIKE YOU.

I PRAY THAT YOU WOULD HEAL _____ HEART.

GIVE _____ A REVELATION OF HOW MUCH YOU LOVE HIM/HER.

GIVE _____ AN EXPERIENCE WITH YOUR LOVE THAT WILL BE LIFE CHANGING, LIFE LOVING, LIFE GIVING AND LIFE WITH YOU IN ETERNITY.

SHOW HIM/HER THROUGH THIS EXPERIENCE YOUR PATIENCE AND KINDNESS, YOUR LONG SUFFERING, AND YOUR GENTLENESS.
SHOW HIM/HER LOVE ISN'T JEALOUS, RUDE, PROUD OR BOASTFUL AND SHOW HIM/HER YOUR LOVE IS NOT DEMANDING. SHOW HIM/HER YOUR LOVE IS FULL OF FORGIVENESS WITH NO HOLDS BARRED AND THAT YOUR LOVE IS UNCONDITIONAL. THEN, OH LORD, GIVE HIM/HER A HEART THAT IS ABLE…TO LOVE LIKE THAT. HELP HIM/HER NAVIGATE THROUGH THE WATERS, WALK THROUGH THE FIRES AND CLIMB THE MOUNTAINS OF LIFE BEING ABLE TO LOVE PEOPLE THAT ARE FLAWED AND MISGUIDED.
HELP HIM/HER TO LOVE EVEN THOSE WHO HARM AND HATE.
HELP HIM/HER GIVE GRACE TO THOSE THAT NEED IT MOST.
THANK YOU, LORD, FOR GIVING HIM/HER A HEART TO LOVE…
LIKE YOU LOVE HIM/HER.
THANK YOU FOR YOUR AMAZING GRACE.
AMEN

Names, Notes and New Things

2-21-20 Father, Thank You for this prayer. I have tried so hard to meet Annie's needs, but what she needs is You. I release her to You. Please take care of her. Please help her to know You and Your love. Thank You.

FROM CLAY'S OWN HAND...
Journal Entry

Thank you Lord for the strength and knowledge you give me everyday.

Dear God, please restore what time I have lost by running from you. Thank you for all that you do for me each and everyday.

PHYSICAL HEALTH

"Dear friend, I pray that you may enjoy good health and that all may go well with you, even as your soul is getting along well." ~ 3 John 1:2

Today we pray for _____ physical health. As addiction has taken a toll on his/her body, we ask you Lord to intervene. We have seen the destructive ways this enemy eats away at _____ body and we ask today, for this to stop. Lord be his/her doctor and his/her dentist. Be everything he/she needs to be whole physically. Heal his/her body inside and out. Let there be nothing left in his/her body from addiction or affliction. Rejuvenate every cell and fiber within him/her. Give life to the dead places and breath to the breathless. If there is any underlying disease or remnant from addictions attack, we ask that you supernaturally repair and heal those places, leaving no trace of any disease or remnant except where those things will be used for his/her highest good. We believe that you Oh Lord are _____ healer. We believe you are able to heal all things. We believe you know _____ physical body better than anyone because you created him/her. Therefore, we believe you are able to bring back your good and perfect work in his/her physical body, for his/her best life. We ask for complete healing. We ask for complete wholeness and we ask for this miracle work to begin right now, today. Thank you, Lord, in advance for allowing us to witness your miraculous healing work, in _____ life.

Amen

Names, Notes and New Things

2-28-20 Father, Annie is so broken. I don't know when/if she has food. Please heal her. She has so many issues. Please make a way where there is no way. Please heal her. Thank You

FROM CLAY'S OWN HAND...
Journal Entry

Lord, as I continue to try and better myself, I pray that you will walk with me in all that I do.

God, whatever things may be hindering me from connecting with you, I pray that they will be visible or if possible removed from my life.

MENTAL HEALTH

"For the mind set on the flesh is death, but the mind set on the Spirit is life and peace." ~Romans 8:6

Lord, we ask today, that _____ mind would be governed by You. We ask today for your heart's desire to rule and reign in his/her mind, will and emotions and that every decision _____ makes would be made with a sound mind, a sober mind, and a mind that operates in truth and love. Lord, we ask that if addiction has rerouted or remapped or rearranged _____ mind in anyway, that you would make it right again. Lord, we ask that you rearrange everything in his/her mind to line up with your perfect destiny and purpose for his/her life. Lord, remove the hands of the enemy from _____ mind and let him/her come to his/her senses. Let him/her see with clarity and give him/her the ability to discern right from wrong and good from evil. Let every decision he/she makes be secured in absolute truth and wisdom. Lord, as your word says, you give wisdom freely when we ask. We are asking. We cry out Lord today for you to pour out your wisdom upon _____ . Hold nothing back from his/her need. Let his/her decisions propel him/her towards righteousness and right standing. Let him/her be known as a man/woman of integrity due to the choices and the decisions he/she makes surrounding not only his/her life, but the lives of every person his/her life touches.

Amen

Names, Notes and New Things

2-23-20 Father, I can't even imagine a time when Annie would be known for her integrity. She has been under addiction's control for so long. But, please let this be so. Someday. Thank 'Em.

FROM CLAY'S OWN HAND...
Journal Entry

Faith is a relationship with God, laying down my will for his.

Lord, please forgive me of my sins and allow me to be more like you, help me as sometimes I am quick to judge and even condemn.

SPIRITUAL HEALTH

"For physical training is of some value, but godliness has value for all things, holding promise for both the present life and the life to come."
~ 1 Timothy 4:8

Lord, we know how much you love _____. You, being his/her creator. Therefore, we ask Lord, pursue him/her. Woo him/her. Stay close. So close that you can even be his/her breath if necessary. Only you God can give the gift of eternal life. We ask you Lord for full redemption in spirit and truth for _____.

Show him/her your master plan to rescue, recover, redeem, and keep him/her for eternity, no matter where he/she has been or what he/she has done. Let him/her have a new revelation of Jesus Christ today. Yes Lord, we pray for a new revelation of redemption and salvation, not an old one, not defined by man or by a church. Let him/her experience brand new for himself/herself, Jesus Christ, alive within him/her. Let him/her experience Your resurrection power and know that it is available to him/her. Today Lord, we ask you to cause this to happen, change the course of every spiritual thing in _____ life that is opposed to You and bring him/her to a place where he/she can see, hear, taste, touch, and even smell the fragrance of Jesus. Today Lord, we ask for _____ salvation. Lord, we ask for a renewal in spirit with all the earth shaking, heaven parting power that was witnessed on the day Jesus was resurrected from the grave. Let this be his/her day to be raised up and set free from every stronghold in his/her life, yes Lord even the stronghold of death that pursues him/her. Today, we speak life over _____, life everlasting. Amen

Names, Notes and New Things

1-23-20

Oh Father, please fill Annie with Your life. Please fill her with Your light. Let it fill every corner, every fiber of her being. Please save her through Your power. Please open their eyes to Your Truth. Please help her get the help she needs. Please bring someone extraordinary into her life. Please get her to treatment TODAY.

In Jesus name

Yeshua
Holy
Lord
Almighty Father
Prince of Peace

FROM CLAY'S OWN HAND...
Journal Entry

Lord, thank you for being with me today, help me to remember to pray for those who have done so much for me, and the ones who are just out to get me.

Lord, I pray if I ever have criticism for another man that you will give me the words to say.

WORDS

"Gentle words bring life and health; a deceitful tongue crushes the spirit." ~Proverbs 15:4

Lord, help _____ guard his/her words. Let him/her not speak words that will trip him/her up. Let the words of his/her mouth and the meditations of his/her heart be pleasing to you. Help him/her understand that the things he/she says from his/her mouth put things into motion around him/her. Let him/her speak good of those in his/her midst. Let him/her encourage those around him/her. Stop him/her from knowingly or unknowingly speaking word curses over people that he/she loves. Stop him/her too from speaking word curses over strangers he/she encounters along the way. Lord, do not allow addiction to control his/her tongue. Help _____ understand that the words he/she chooses to speak, have power and that they move everyone and everything they touch. Do not allow him/her to set a trap for himself/herself through conversations. We ask that you stop his/her talk with the enemy and guard his/her heart. Cause _____ to think on those things that will be helpful to him/her and meditate on things that will encourage him/her, therefore producing help and encouragement to all those he/she encounters. Let _____ be known as a helper, and an encourager and one who lifts the spirits of those around him/her with every word he/she speaks. Give him/her a new understanding of the power of the spoken word!

Amen

Names, Notes and New Things

1-24-20 Father Annie says & posts such filthy things. It breaks my heart and gives me such anxiety. I have the darkness in her. Please fill her with Your light. Please help her to desire You. Please flood every corner of her being with Your light. Please bring someone who is extraordinary into her life and show her that You love her & she is worthy.

FROM CLAY'S OWN HAND...
Journal Entry

Dear Lord, I ask that you would empower me to carry out your commands needed to move on with my life.

Choose not to be offended, interact with others in a way that is pleasing to God, remain humble, pray for wisdom and ask for God to bring resolution and clarity to all situations.

ENVIRONMENT
"Bad company corrupts good character" ~1 Corinthians 15:33

Keep _____ Oh Lord from perverse places. Keep him/her out of the presence of those who are practicing lawlessness and abuse. Change his/her direction if he/she sets out for a place that he/she doesn't need to be, even if it is home or work with family or friends. Let him/her not be tempted to hang out with people that will aid and abet the enemy in entrapment. With eyes to see and ears to hear, give him/her a heightened awareness of everyone and everything going on around him/her. Cause _____ to see the deceptive practices of those who give him/her invitations into dark places that are filled with temptation. Guard him/her from the wiles of the enemy that tries to deceive him/her into traps. Cause him/her to be aware of even those things in the air, in the atmosphere that can woo him/her into the enemy's camp. Cause him/her to carefully discern conversations, media and music at all times. Let him/her see the motive behind each of these so that he/she can easily identify deceptive practices and harmful temptations. Pour out your wisdom Oh Lord upon _____ and allow him/her the ability to govern his/her body, mind and soul, keeping him/her from entering a place that has been set as a trap of temptation. Cause him/her to be vigilant and aware of his/her surroundings at all times. And Lord, if he/she finds himself/herself in a trap, let _____ see clearly, you have made a WAY out!
Amen

Names, Notes and New Things

2-26-20 Oh Father, please open Annie's eyes to the dangers of the people she is drawn to, the music she listens to, the shows she watches (when she is not homeless). Please help her to have discernment and to turn from everything and everyone who does not dwell in Your light. Help her to seek Your light. Thank You, Lord.

FROM CLAY'S OWN HAND...
Journal Entry

Lord, I thank you for your mercy and grace and for pulling me out of the hole that I have been digging for years. Only you are capable of such things, I ask that you would empower me to continue down the path you have created for me.

God set up perimeters that I could not cross in order to guide me down his narrow path.

SAFETY

"But the Lord is faithful, and He will strengthen you and protect you from the evil one." ~2 Thessalonians 3:3

We say again, _____ belongs to YOU Jesus. We ask you Father to cover _____ by the blood of Jesus and encamp your angels around him/her. We know Lord that you send angels to fight for your very own and we ask now for you to send your angel army to fight for _____ safety. We pray that not one hair on his/her head could be touched by harm and that you hem him/her into your boundaries. Draw a line Lord that no enemy can cross and no matter where he/she goes, let the enemy be warned that he has no rights to him/her. Show _____ your angels. Show _____ your mighty right hand. Show _____ your intervention on his/her behalf so that he/she will know you are for him/her and not against him/her. If he/she is cold, give him/her warmth, if he/she is hungry, send food to fill his/her stomach. If he/she is lonely, wrap him/her in your arms and send a Godly companion until this time passes. If he/she is in danger of falling into any form of trap or snare set by the enemy, move _____ , Lord, do not let his/her foot come near danger. Save him/her Lord even from his/her own plans. Keep him/her Lord as long as it takes to bring him/her to safety. Thank you, God, for fulfilling every need and making every provision for _____ safe passage.

Amen

Names, Notes and New Things

1-29-20
Lord, it hurts so much to see the path Annie has chosen. It is so dangerous and she seems so happy there. I hate this! Please, Father bring Godly people into her life. Please help her to get help. Thank you that you are greater than this. It seems so hopeless.

FROM CLAY'S OWN HAND...
Journal Entry

Jesus, I want to move forward with my life.

I believe he reached out to me to reach others through my understanding through him, not my own.

PEOPLE

"Greater love has no one than this, to lay down one's life for a friend." ~John 15:13

Lord, send your people to _____ . Let him/her recognize those that are full of Your light. Help him/her quickly recognize those that are on assignment from darkness. Help _____ choose good and faithful people to be in relationship with. Help him/her choose wisely what family, friends and co-workers are good and full of integrity, and those that will walk beside him/her in truth. Help_____ , gravitate towards good people and avoid those that wish him/her harm. Show him/her those with selfish motives and vain intentions and separate him/her from those people. Cause him/her to see with the mind of Christ those that have been chosen by you and hold fast to those who show him/her the love of Christ in all they say and do.

Lord, help _____ see the good in others. Help him/her locate the Jesus in them and use wisdom when choosing who he/she will spend time with. Lord we ask you to create a divine separation from those that mean _____ harm and create a divine pursuit towards those that you have placed in his/her life for kinship, community, protection and help. Lord, move _____ into the relationships that you have pre-destined for him/her. Sever every tie that binds him/her to unhealthy people. Break every soul tie meant for harm. Shine your light into every relationship for _____ highest good. Help him/her choose good friends and help him/her be that same good friend. Amen

Names, Notes and New Things

1/30/20

Father, You know that Annie seeks out people who are dark and hurtful. Why has she always been drawn to those who walk in darkness? Please change her heart. Please let that small crack of light enter her heart & flow to fullness. Please hurry godly people into her life & help her to be attracted to them and repelled from the others instead of the opposite. Please fill her with Your light. Please cast out the demons in her & replace them with Your Holy Spirit. Father, I release her today to Your loving care and tender mercies. Please work today to heal her and save her.

FROM CLAY'S OWN HAND...
Journal Entry

When tempted, I will turn to God for my answer and pray for peace about the situation.

Dear God, help me to be forgiving, as you are and to become stronger in my faith in you everyday.

RECOVERY PROGRAMS

"Don't believe every spirit but test the spirits to see whether they are from God, because many false prophets have gone out into the world."
~John 4:1

Lord, as we walk this journey, we seem to take hold of anything and everything that we think can *save* in the wake of this storm called addiction. Help us!

Help _____ choose wisely the programs that will help him/her. Those that teach truth and produce life. Steer him/her away from those that will cause harm and are in opposition to your plan and purpose.

Let him/her get help in those places that you have deemed helpful and guard him/her from those places whose agenda does not line up with yours. Help _____ avoid programs that are led by people with their own agendas and seek only fame or financial gain from this plague of addiction. Shut every door that opens into an unhealthy environment. Stop him/her from entering programs that would cause further damage and prolong recovery. Put up immoveable roadblocks to stop _____ from entering a program that is not perfectly aligned with your plan and established with a right heart. Let their motivation be love. We ask you Lord, to remove every obstacle for entrance into the program(s) you choose. Let his/her path be straight and provision made, into programs that align with Your plan for complete deliverance from the stronghold of addiction.

Amen

Names, Notes and New Things

1-31-20

Father, You know Annie's heart right now, she doesn't want treatment. She wants to be "free". Please change her heart and help her get the help she needs. Please open a door to the right treatment place and close every other door, including the door to remaining a homeless addict. Please Father, put her where she needs to be.

FROM CLAY'S OWN HAND...
JOURNAL ENTRY

MERCY, GRACE AND FORGIVENESS ARE GIVEN TO US BY GOD SO THAT WE MAY GIVE THE SAME TO OTHERS.

THE MOST EFFECTIVE WAY TO HANDLE CONFLICT IS THROUGH PRAYER.

JOBS

"All things work together for the good, for those who love God."
~Romans 8:28

Lord, as _____ navigates the wake of addiction, help him/her find employment that will support healthy recovery. Show him/her employers that will understand his/her circumstances, the wake of legal issues, the mental and emotional stress he/she faces and the time needed to purse recovery in a healthy environment. Make a way Oh Lord for _____ to be able to find a job that will allow grace for appointments, meetings and family time as needed to repair broken relationships and uphold obligations to courts, recovery programs, family and friends. We ask you Lord to open doors that would allow _____ to receive uncommon favor and that you would provide finances through a healthy work environment that would allow him/her to manage and meet the responsibilities that he/she has committed to. Thank you in advance Lord for business owners, managers and co-workers that understand the journey of addiction and that are purposed to be helpful in the rebuilding of _____ life and helpful in giving opportunity. Thank you for an environment of respect in the pursuit of building a healthy community. A community that extends from the workplace to the home. Lord, help _____ see your hand in every provision and let him/her know, you are there, as the right doors are opened, and the wrong doors are closed. Show _____ that you really can make a way where there seems to be no way. Amen

Names, Notes and New Things

2-1-20 Father, it seems odd to pray for a job for Annie. She doesn't want one. She wants to be free from all responsibilities — to not have to worry about anything or anyone — I guess she worries about how she will get drugs - but in my mind that is all and that is what she wants. Please change her. She says it's her life & she can live it the way she wants. I can't even imagine. Please make a way when there seem to be no way. Please make a stream through the wilderness. Please change her heart. Help her to be tired of all this and fulfill the plan you have for her.

Thank you for the work you are doing that I cannot see. Please help me to see.

FROM CLAY'S OWN HAND...
Journal Entry

Lord, as I continue to press further and closer to you, allow me to be slow to anger and negativity.

Lord, grant me humility in times of pride and your gift of forgiveness.

PRIDE

"Clothe yourself with humility." ~1 Peter 5:5

Lord, I pray that you will help _____ know and understand that he/she is not in this place alone. Help him/her see, know and understand that he/she is not the only one who has fallen prey to this attack. Explain to him/her that this battle cannot be fought or won alone and that he/she is not capable of overcoming the giants in the land of addiction without help, first and foremost, your help. Show him/her Oh Lord that you have placed an army of people in his/her midst to help him/her. Take away the thought that he/she can do this on his/her own. Help him/her lay down the false pretense and mindset of "I can do this by myself" and embrace the help that you have sent to him/her. By your Spirit, show him/her those you have placed in his/her life to give him/her help, refuge and hope. Help him/her readily accept help from all good and Godly people. Show him/her the places in his/her life where pride is attached, so that he/she can have a full and complete release from the effects of pride in mind, heart, soul and spirit. Help _____ humbly submit to the understanding that you have created him/her for a good purpose with an eternal destiny. Help him/her understand that you alone bring good from evil and beauty from ashes. Help him/her lay everything at your feet Oh Lord. Take all selfish pride from his/her life and replace it with humility. Cause Oh Lord, _____ to completely surrender to YOU, his/her creator. Jesus, the One who loves him/her most.
Amen

Names, Notes and New Things

2-2-20

Father, here we are at another Sunday. I am sad and defeated. I ask You again to send a battalion of angels to Annie to help, save and protect her. I ask that You would open her heart & mind to getting help. She cannot do this alone and right now, she doesn't want to change. Please help her to truly want to change and lead her to a place where she can get help.

Thank You

FROM CLAY'S OWN HAND...
Journal Entry

Dear Lord, as I practice being more like you, I pray for wisdom, knowledge and understanding to carry out the things that you have ask of me.

Pray for wisdom, knowledge and understanding in all situations.

TRUST

"Trust in the Lord with all your heart and lean not on your own understanding, in all your ways acknowledge Him and He will direct your path." ~Proverbs 3:5

In the wake of anger, bitterness, resentment, judgement, unforgiveness, blame, shame, guilt and lack of trust…

Lord, help "me" trust You.
Lord, help _____ trust You.

Reach through the issues of life and let _____ experience your LOVE. Let him/her experience your love with every part of his/her being, drawing him/her to trust in You. Let this experience open his/her heart to trust that You are real and that You have always been with him/her. Let him/her experience the revelation truth that you are his/her creator and that from the moment of creation, You have never left his/her side. Do what only you can do Oh Lord, remove the veil from his/her eyes and heart. Reveal to him/her who You are, so that he/she will be compelled to TRUST YOU. Cause _____ to recognize he/she has been given a gift of faith and cause him/her to exercise that gift NOW! Pierce the cloak of addiction Lord, remove the veil of deception! Rush in with the gift of FAITH!
Cause him/her to TRUST in You with all his/her heart and lean not on his/her own understanding.
Amen

Names, Notes and New Things

2-3-20 Please Father help Annie and me to trust in You. Please provide for all her needs. Please help her to see You and to know that You have never left her. Help her to know that Your plans for her are good. Please help her get the help she needs! Thank You Abba Father.

FROM CLAY'S OWN HAND...
Journal Entry

Dear Lord, please allow me to rid myself of the character defects and resentments that I have held for so long.

Lord, grant me the patience to forgive others and to not be so quick to anger.

CHURCH

"For where two or three are gathered together in my name, I am in the midst of them." ~Matthew 18:20

Lord, help us understand that *we are the church* and that it does not reside within four walls.

Establish _____ faith in You. Show him/her a family of God that will love him/her like Jesus.

Show him/her that there is a family of God that loves unconditionally and welcomes him/her, just as he/she is. Give wisdom, insight and understanding to _____ as he/she seeks fellowship with other believers in Christ so that he/she will not get entangled in a "church" system that is destined for failure. Remove all false teaching and false doctrine that may have been imposed upon him/her as a child or adolescent and replace those things with truth.
Help _____ understand that the church is to be a temple of holiness and goodness, established in love. Help him/her understand that people have flaws and that misguided and hurting people hurt people. Show him/her Oh Lord, this is where grace comes in.
Help him/her find a church family that is established in the love of Jesus. Help _____ love You with all his/her heart and others as himself/herself. Help him/her understand this love relationship and that people, not buildings are the church. Help him/her find a gathering place that worships in Spirit and Truth!
Amen

Names, Notes and New Things

2-4-20 Please Father replace the darkness in Annie with Your light. She is running so hard away from You. She has always been tempted by & drawn to the darkness. Please flood her life with Your light. Please draw her toward godly people. Please replace her desire for the love of a man with a desire for Your love. Help her to know that she is forgiven. That she is a new creation in Christ. Please cleanse and heal her and make her whole. Help her to love herself.
Thank You Father.

FROM CLAY'S OWN HAND...
Journal Entry

Lord, as I ask for forgiveness from others, please give me patience when needed, and give me the proper words to convey humbleness in asking.

Follow God's instruction and you will have greater peace.

DECEPTION

"Be not deceived, God is not mocked, for whatever a man or woman sows, that they shall also reap." ~Galatians 6:7

Oh Lord, we need your insight. We have been deceived by so many things in the day we live in. Help us Oh Lord to see every issue with your eyes so that we may not be deceived.

Lord, we pray that you will sever the ties of deception over _____ mind, heart and soul. We pray You would intervene in the working of deception within every part of _____ life. Shine your light of truth into every area that has had a cloak of deception thrown over it. Let nothing go without your attention Oh God! We cry out for intervention. Make every crooked path straight and remove every lie perpetrated upon _____ mind. Reveal every lie that has been assigned to him/her physically, mentally, emotionally and spiritually. Let this revelation turn on the light where it has been turned off and reveal to _____ that without him/her knowing, deception and addiction have clouded, misguided, turned, pulled, pursued and rerouted his/her thoughts, words and his/her actions. Be the revelator today Oh Lord, reveal the deception that has tried to steal, kill and destroy _____ life. And Lord, please reveal any deception in my life too. Do not let me be duped by my own understanding of anything! I choose to live in truth, just as I am asking that you make a way for _____ to live in truth.

Amen

Names, Notes and New Things

2-5-20 Father, this prayer is so true and necessary. Annie has been deceived for so long by drugs and alcohol. They have lied to her, telling her that she needs them to make her feel better. She is so messed up. I don't even know if she is alive. Please shine the light of your truth into both of our lives. Satan is telling me that you don't care and prayer doesn't help. For he it, from me that I should sin against you by ceasing to pray for her.

FROM CLAY'S OWN HAND...
Journal Entry

Lord, be with me as me and my family rekindle you as the bridge between us.

Try to live honest.

FAMILY
"For where your treasure is, there will your heart be also."
~Luke 12:34

Jesus, our family needs you. We need your grace and your mercy. We need rest. We need understanding, where we cannot understand, we need you to intervene in our decisions, where we have gone astray, and for you to correct the decisions that we have made in error. We need you Jesus to speak to the storm. We need your help to believe. Oh Lord, help our unbelief! Show us your light in dark places. We need physical, emotional and spiritual strength to keep going and the endurance to finish the race. Lord, repair all the broken relationships brought about by the chaos of addiction. We pray that you will reconcile every mother and father, brother and sister, grandparents, spouses, children and other family members. Reconcile these broken relationships Oh Lord. We know you made us to live in love and your desire is for us to cherish each other. Help _____ forgive us all and help all of us, forgive him/her. Help us Oh Lord to choose good and healthy words and actions. Help us understand that your word, as it is written will not return void and help us walk by faith and not by sight. Help us call those things which are not, as though they are and help us to keep our eyes on the eternal things even when there is a storm raging all around us here on earth. Remind us Oh Lord, that the waves and wind still know your name. We ask you to speak to the storm! Peace... be still! Show us Lord, love wins. Amen

Names, Notes and New Things

2-6-20 Father, please heal & repair our family. Help us to love and forgive each other, especially Annie. Her sibs do not like her. She is so selfish & has caused so much pain. Please help me to have faith & hope & call it as it is. Help me to always carry my umbrella, believing that prayer works & You are faithful & will keep Your promises. Thank You.

FROM CLAY'S OWN HAND...
Journal Entry

Lord, I pray that you will give my family peace of mind about where I am and my situation with the law.

Forgive and you will be forgiven.

LEGAL ISSUES

"...IF ANYONE DOES SIN, WE HAVE AN ADVOCATE WITH THE FATHER, JESUS CHRIST, THE RIGHTEOUSNESS." ~1John 2:1

As we approach the throne of grace on behalf of _____, we ask Oh God that you establish yourself as _____ advocate. You are our highest authority and we ask that you, today, hold the heart of the judge (king) in your hand. Lord, we pray for mercy and we pray for grace. Lord, we pray, thy will be done. We ask that you make yourself known to _____ so that he/she will be comforted, knowing he/she has representation. Move the people, paperwork, finances and circumstances into order for your perfect will. Lord, we ask that _____ would have a repentant heart, when needed. We pray he/she have a full understanding of what he/she is facing as a result of any charge held against him/her. Lord, help _____ see clearly his/her position. Oh God! Don't let him/her miss the lesson in this season so that he/she would not have to revisit judgement or imprisonment, regardless of his/her guilt or innocence.
If imprisonment is necessary, give him/her supernatural endurance and protection that causes him/her to see you are with him/her in all things.
Oh God, let _____ see you walk through walls! Show up in people, places and things. Be his/her great physician if he/she becomes in need of medical or dental care and speak to him/her so that he/she is fully aware that you are there. Stay his/her mind on you Lord! We ask you to pour Your justice into this place, knowing You are full of mercy, grace and love. Amen

Names, Notes and New Things

2-7-20 Father, You know Annie's legal issues now + all those to come. She is running from them + I will impact her life if she doesn't face them. Please help her to think clearly about her future and help her to do what is right. Father, she is doing illegal things now. I pray that Your will be done as far as her being caught. I don't know what is right, but You do. Please watch over her + let Your will be done in her life. Thank You, Lord

FROM CLAY'S OWN HAND...
Journal Entry

Dear Lord, I pray that you will be with me throughout this week and whatever obstacles that I may encounter that you will help me see things for what they are.

If I offend others, I will apologize and try to resolve the issue.

CHILDREN

"Jesus said, let the little children come to me, do not hinder them, for of such is the kingdom of heaven." ~Matthew 19:14

(For your child or their children)

Oh, gracious God! Please be with the little ones and our older ones alike, children that are affected by the chaos of addiction. We pray that you would be the good, good Father & Mother that every child needs. Lord, be their All in All!

Where there have been lies perpetrated on their minds, we ask you to speak truth into their spirits, truth that corrects! Where there has been abuse and neglect, we ask you to speak healing to every part of their being, even to the marrow of their bones! We pray Lord that every need is met by You through this season and that You are working now to restore broken relationships caused by abuse, neglect, deception and lack of love. Oh Lord, restore and reconcile every moment the enemy has stolen! Thank you for being a redeemer of time!

Above all, Lord show every child how much you love them, like only you can, their Creator & Heavenly Father.
Abba Father... let them know how much they are loved! Be an all-consuming fire to the hearts and minds of every child affected by addiction.

Amen

Names, Notes and New Things

2-8-20 Oh, Father, please help Annie to understand thy greatness of Your love for her. Please relentlessly pursue her. Please send out an army to rescue her. Please reach her where I can't.
Thank You

FROM CLAY'S OWN HAND...
JOURNAL ENTRY

DO NOT SEEK REVENGE, LEAVE IT IN GOD'S HANDS.

GOD ALONE HAS THE POWER TO JUDGE.

EMOTIONS

"Trust in the Lord with all your heart, and do not lean on your own understanding. In all your ways acknowledge him, and he will make straight your paths." ~ Prov. 3:5-6

Lord of all creation, we pray that you would help us with our emotions. Help us to walk in harmony with your purpose and will for our lives. Lord, you know _____ better than anyone! You know what he/she has been through in every season of his/her life. You alone know what drives the emotions he/she contends with. It is you alone who can help!

Lord, we pray that you will speak to every negative emotion that rises up within _____. We ask you to stop that emotion from causing him/her to be moved towards danger or deception. Cause _____ to recognize quickly that which he/she contends with and give him/her the ability to navigate through troubled waters to a safe place, a place of refuge and right standing, a place of safety.

Lord, we ask that you impart peace to _____ that penetrates to the depths of his/her soul. Give him/her a peace that is the well from which he/she draws his/her response to every circumstance. Remove forever the harmful emotions of the past and establish a peaceful response forever and ever. Let _____ know you have intervened in every emotion and that you have chosen peace on his/her behalf.
Amen

NAMES, NOTES AND NEW THINGS

2-9-20 Lord, this is so right for today. I am seeing how damaged Annie is and has been for a long time. Whatever happened to her when she was young caused great damage. She is seeking love & acceptance in all the wrong places & almost always has. Please heal her & help her get the help she needs. If it is Your will, please give her long term care somewhere, somehow. Please make her receptive to Your light. She is full of darkness. Please send someone to share Your light with her. Thank You

FROM CLAY'S OWN HAND...
Journal Entry

Lord, please allow me to know you better so that one day I can be with you.

The reward I expect from him is his saving Grace and to be with him in heaven.

ADDICTION

No temptation has overtaken you except what is common to mankind. And God is faithful; he will not let you be tempted beyond what you can bear. But when you are tempted, he will also provide a way out so that you can endure it. ~ 1 Corinthians 10:13-14

Oh Lord, we declare you faithful to see and know what _____ contends with. When _____ is tempted with the desires and cravings of addiction, please provide a way out so that he/she may endure until he/she reaches safety and has peace of mind. We pray that you would intervene in any and every form of addiction that has laid hold of _____ mind, his/her heart, his/her soul and his/her body. Lord invade his/her spirit that he/she would have the ability to overcome this thing that has been in pursuit of his/her life.

Sever the hold, sever the tie, sever any and all relationships that promote this destructive adversary. Lord, according to Your Word, we declare that this battle belongs to You and we trust your ability to overcome this thing called "addiction".

Help us see through Your eyes Oh Lord, the victory at hand, the impossible made possible. the mighty right hand of God moving in our midst! We trust your eternal plan and purpose for _____.

THY WILL BE DONE

Amen

Names, Notes and New Things

2-10-20 Father please break the hold of Drugs, alcohol + Sex on Annie. Please sever the ties of all the destructive things in her life. Please help to get the help that she needs. Please forgive me for underestimating Your Power.
Thank You.

I pray that through this, your heart learns to sing again...
When you surrender all that has happened, your soul will be moved.

Oh, when I pray, something happens!
Oh, when I say, I'm not in control
When I surrender, all that's happened
Something moves down in my soul...

You are not alone!
Even when you can't pray...
We are here.
We are praying.

"Lord, intervene and deliver us to peace!"

Even when you can't pray...
God hears your heart!

A few weeks after Clay went to heaven, I was driving down the road with tears streaming down my face, missing him like crazy. And suddenly...I felt "a wave of peace". It was him saying, "Momma, everything's gonna be ok". I am certain, with no doubt.
God heard my heart. He knew my need. He answered! God hears your heart too!

In loving memory of:
Joseph Clay Iaquinta

Clay entered heaven December 21, 2018 at 24 years old.

Clay made it known that he believed Jesus was who He said He was. He had a ministry of presence and was not shy about sharing his faith. We have no doubt that Clay is with Jesus. We are certain that we will see him again.

He loved out loud and never met a stranger. He entered relationships on purpose and cared deeply for the people he encountered. He carried his brother's burden.

…and yes, Clay struggled with addiction and everything that goes along with it. Clay would want you to know that addiction does not define someone's heart and who they are. It is a force to be reckoned with, yet even in the moment of death, the light of Jesus Christ overcomes the darkest dark. Jesus intervened.

Clay's life motto was:

"Friend of Love"
"Any friend of love…is a friend of mine."

I share this knowing his story is so much like so many others, in hope that you know, you are not alone.

CLOSING

Written by: Shannon Stockstill

Clay had an eye on heaven in worship, and saw in the spiritual what gift was ahead. Jesus knew he needed this gift more than he needed this temporary life.

"Precious in the sight of the LORD is the death of his saints." *Psalm 116:15* Let them motivate us to live a life worthy of God's calling. Let their past faithfulness propel us to do the same in the present.

I pray we allow the earthly death of our Clayboy to have even more impact on our lives. Let his going home galvanize our faith. Clay never abandoned his love for Jesus. He remained faithful to the end. His life of perseverance and his love for Jesus is a tremendous motivation for us to do the same.

His influence is so much greater from heaven than on earth. I pray that God will graft Clay's passion for His word into our hearts and minds. Now in his earthly death, he has heaven's platform for even greater Kingdom leverage.

Glossary of Terms

Atmosphere - the pervading tone or mood of a place or situation

Abundance - plenty of the good things of life, prosperity

Addiction - dependency, habit, fixation, enslavement

Battle - a lengthy and difficult conflict or struggle

Deception - the action of deceiving someone, lying, fraud

Destiny - what is meant to be, a divine decree, future

Divisive - tending to cause disagreement or hostility between people

Emotions - a strong feeling from circumstances and mood

Environment - surroundings or conditions where a person operates

Forgiveness - the action or process of being forgiven, to pardon, to give mercy

Grace - unmerited favor, divine assistance, help from God as well as others, support, kindness

Humility - humble, lowliness, meek, to recognize your value and another's value while looking up

Intercession - the action of intervening on behalf of another, prayer

Knowledge - awareness gained by experience, perception, realization

Legal - Having to do with the law, natural law and spiritual law, decree, rule, measure, covenant

Mercy - compassion shown to someone to whom it is within your ability to punish or harm

Miracle - a highly improbable or extraordinary event that brings a welcoming outcome, one that is not explainable in natural law

Misguided - having or showing faulty judgement or reasoning

Opposition - resistance or dissent, expressed in action or argument

Overwhelming - very great amount, massive, formidable, devastating

Perpetrated - to carry out or commit a harmful, illegal or immoral action

Perspective - a point of view, an attitude towards something

Pride - a feeling of satisfaction found in one's own achievements

Purpose - the reason for which something is done or created or for which something or someone exists

Rejuvenate - restore, revitalize, renew

Reproof - an expression of blame or disapproval

Righteousness - a quality of being morally right or justifiable

Safety - the position of being protected from danger, risk or injury

Soul - mind, will and emotions

Spirit – heart, where our core beliefs reside

Surrender - the action of surrendering, cease resistance

Trust - believing in the reliability, truth and ability of strength of something or in someone, can also be likened to faith

Vigilant - keeping careful watch for possible danger or difficulty

Wake - a trail of disturbance, turbulence

Unforgiveness - the inability to let go of an offense towards someone who has harmed or offended you

Note: There are multiple definitions for some words. I have included the ones that best describe the purpose and intent of this work, in relation to our position to God, each other and ourselves.

There is a recovery series titled:
Recovery…Discovery
(Set of 3 Workbooks)

The 2nd in the series was written & dedicated to Clay.

"Come and See…Yourself in Me"

You will find this workbook series available at:
www.amazon.com
(search by author's name)
Authors: Wendell VanValin and Shannon Stockstill

Book 1: The Path…Getting Started
Book 2: Come and See…Yourself in Me
Book 3: Hit'n the Street…Life after Rehab

These workbooks were written to be used in a group recovery setting. They are not bible studies or self-help books. They are designed for one to find the authentic version of themselves while living in community.

For more information contact: cheryl.iaquinta@aol.com

GRACE AND PEACE BE YOURS IN ABUNDANCE
THROUGH THE KNOWLEDGE OF GOD AND OF
JESUS OUR LORD.

2 PETER 1:2 NIV